SEA
DISASTERS

Rhoda Nottridge

Thomson Learning
New York

BOOKS IN THIS SERIES

AIR DISASTERS

ENVIRONMENTAL DISASTERS

NATURAL DISASTERS

SEA DISASTERS

Cover Photographs:
(Background) The power and danger of the sea should always be respected by sea travelers.
(Inset) The horror of being trapped on a blazing oil rig in the North Sea had to be faced by the crew on board the Piper Alpha *oil rig when it exploded on July 6, 1988.*

First published in the
United States in 1993 by
Thomson Learning
115 Fifth Avenue
New York, NY 10003

First published in 1993 by
Wayland (Publishers) Ltd.

Cataloging-in-Publication Data applied for

ISBN 1-56847-084-3

Printed in Italy

CONTENTS

FROM CANOES TO PASSENGER LINERS

Water makes up nearly three-quarters of Earth's surface, covering one million, three hundred-thousand square miles. The sea is one of nature's most magnificent and powerful forces.

The sea has many moods. In one place, it will gently lick a child's toes as she wades at the beach. Elsewhere in the world, it will be raging in a storm, throwing up waves 60 feet high. One thing is certain—the power of the sea must always be respected. Though it gives us food to eat and carries us around the world, the sea can also kill us.

Humans have been building craft to travel the seas for over 5,000 years. The ancient Egyptians created some early examples. The first Egyptian boats might have been made from just a few pieces of wood or bundles of reeds tied together, with some animal skins filled with air to keep them afloat.

By 3000 B.C. the Egyptians had started to use sails. Later, other great civilizations such as the Greeks and Romans made bigger and better boats.

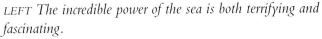

LEFT *The incredible power of the sea is both terrifying and fascinating.*
BELOW *This drawing shows the design of a an Egyptian reed boat.*

SHIPWRECK DISCOVERIES

In the time of the Roman Empire, hundreds of ships sailed around the Mediterranean Sea, bringing the Romans all kinds of goods from foreign countries.

The ships made their owners fabulously wealthy, but there was a price to be paid. Sometimes a sudden storm with huge waves would tear a ship apart. The cargo and crew would sink to the seabed.

In recent years the wreck of a Roman trading ship was salvaged by marine geologist Robert Ballard. He named the ship the *Isis*. Although no one knows the true fate of the *Isis*, Ballard believes that in about A.D. 400 the ship was caught up in a storm, the crew was drowned, and the cargo was lost.

LEFT *Divers have been exploring sea wrecks for centuries – in search of lost treasure or looking for secrets from the past.*

OPPOSITE *The Vikings used their sailing skills to explore new lands.*

The seabed was too deep for divers to be able to reach the wreck. A modern underwater robot made it possible to find the wreck of the *Isis* on the seabed and salvage some of its cargo. It was a fascinating discovery.

The Romans carried much of their cargoes of food in huge clay jars. After the underwater robot had brought up some jars from the shipwreck, the clay that they were made from was tested. It was possible to discover from the tests that some of the jars had contained olive oil and others fish paste.

The shape of these clay storage jars and the type of lamps used by the Romans changed according to the fashion of the times. It was possible to use these salvaged items to find out when the ship was built and used. An ancient shipwreck like the *Isis* can tell historians and archeologists all sorts of things about Roman trading ships, which add to their understanding of this ancient civilization.

VIKING EXPLORERS TO TRADE SHIPS

Boats such as the Viking longships were open, wooden sailing vessels. From around A.D. 800 to A.D. 1000, these great ships were used to fight, trade, and explore Europe and even North America, making the Vikings the most advanced sailors of their time.

By the thirteenth century, warships had been developed that had "castles"—covered sections built on the boats. Sailors experimented by using three main sails and masts instead of one, with extra smaller sails to catch as much of the wind traveling across the ship as possible. This made sailing much faster.

In the fifteenth and sixteenth centuries, sailing ships excelled as the best method of exploring faraway lands. The risks of sea travel were great—there were many disasters and many people died. Yet for bold European adventurers, the lure of possible wealth waiting for them in unknown lands far outweighed any danger. They sailed on, trading with and stealing from the peoples of the new lands they found.

ABOVE *Since the* Mary Rose *was raised from the mud in 1982, she has been kept in a museum in Portsmouth, England. The wooden wreck is kept moist by water sprays so that the wood does not fall apart.*

LEFT *A diagram showing how the* Mary Rose *looked when she was built in 1545.*

A TUDOR TRAGEDY

The *Mary Rose* was an English warship in the sixteenth century. She was the pride of a fleet of warships built for King Henry VIII and was named after his sister. In July 1545, the *Mary Rose* set sail with the fleet to do battle against the French navy, which was trying to attack England.

Watched by King Henry, the English navy began to move out of Portsmouth harbor on the southern coast of England.

Suddenly, a terrible disaster struck. For no known reason, the *Mary Rose* began to sink very quickly. Around 600 sailors died, since there was no time to get off the ship.

On the seabed, the boat was soon covered by a layer of mud. About 20 years ago the great ship was found by sea divers. Many items on the ship had been protected by the mud. The skeletons of some of the sailors still wore the leather shoes and jackets they had put on more than 400 years ago.

ABOVE *This beautifully decorated clay jug was one of the many items recovered in good condition from the wreck of the* Mary Rose.

In October 1982, the wreckage of the *Mary Rose* was lifted from the seabed. We have learned a lot about life on a Tudor sailing ship from the remains that the mud preserved so well. From hair combs to musical instruments, the mud held more than 14,000 objects from the past.

LESSONS TO BE LEARNED

Shipbuilding continued to advance in the centuries after the Age of Exploration. By the mid-nineteenth century, greater understanding of ship design led to the development of the clipper. Built for speed, clippers made trading voyages between Europe, Asia, and the Americas in record time.

At the same time, steamships were being built. In 1843, the first ocean-going steamship, called the *Great Britain*, was launched. It sailed regularly between England and Australia. Unlike the sailing ships, steamships did not rely on the wind and weather conditions.

Engines improved steadily. The coal-burning engines of the first steamships were replaced by better oil-burning ones. As steam travel became more sophisticated, huge ocean liners were built. Eventually the diesel engine became the most common method of driving a big ship. Today, ships with diesel engines can travel at over 60 mph.

For every extraordinary advance that has been made in shipbuilding, unfortunately there have been mistakes too. The larger the vessel, the larger the scale of the disaster that can happen.

There are many natural disasters that have occurred when ships have been struck by very bad weather conditions and other hazards of the deep. It is clear that the sea is a powerful force that demands great respect.

The seabed is also the resting place for many vessels that sank, not because they have been claimed by the forces of nature,

but because of human error. For every dreadful sea disaster that takes place, there are lessons to be learned. We must try to improve the safety of sea vessels to prevent such tragedies from ever happening again.

ABOVE *The magnificent ocean liner* Queen Elizabeth 2 *takes thousands of people each year on magnificent cruise vacations. She is pictured here in 1969 at the English port of Southampton. The ship had a good safety record until August 1992, when she ran aground. No ship is completely safe.*

DISASTER IN THE DEPTHS

The great inventor Leonardo da Vinci is said to have worked out a design for a submarine in the thirteenth century but refused to show it to anyone because he thought it could be put to evil uses. Although some submarines are used for scientific underwater exploration by research groups, most submarines in operation around the world belong to different countries' navies. Submarines are generally used to carry out secret missions for the governments that own them.

It is difficult to know how many submarines have disappeared in the depths of the sea. The public does not often hear about submarines sinking. Many countries keep quiet about their underwater activities because they use submarines to spy on other nations' ships. If a submarine gets into trouble while on a secret mission, the navy that owns the vessel may not be able to tell the public—especially if the tragedy happens during wartime.

However, in 1939, a disaster happened that was certainly not kept quiet—it shocked the world.

TRAPPED UNDERWATER

The *Thetis* was a new submarine that was being tested on June 2, 1939 in the sea close to the north coast of Wales. An unusually large number of people were on board the submarine. They were guests invited to inspect this new addition to the British Navy.

Because the submarine had not been officially handed over to the navy by its builders, the *Thetis* was only accompanied by a tugboat called *Grebecock*, instead of the usual navy escort ship. The *Grebecock*'s job

ABOVE The Thetis *was taking its first test dive when it sank with 103 men on board. The stern of the submarine was spotted the next morning.*

OPPOSITE In a powerful, modern submarine, sailors can remain underwater for several months because of better air supply technology.

BELOW Reports in newspapers at the time gave little hope for the rescue of the men trapped on board the stricken Thetis.

.URDAY, ⌐ &ail, JUN.

THETIS: "HOPE ABANDONED" STATEMENT THIS MORNING

Fear Tide Capsized Submarine After All-day Rescue Attempts

IN PERIL FOR OTHERS

THIS vivid *Daily Mail* picture of the drama off Great Orme's Head shows a salvage worker making his perilous way up the stern of the Thetis in an effort to make fast a hawser. A little later a strong tide caused the submarine to cant and her "tail to go under water." Note the anxious watchers in the bow of the ship on the right.

"TAPPING BRINGS NO REPLY" REPORT

THERE is "no hope" of saving the men still imprisoned in the submarine Thetis. This grave announcement was made at Messrs. Cammell Lairds shipyard at Birkenhead this morning.

Ninety-four men were on board the vessel when she sank. Four escaped yesterday morning by means of the Davis apparatus— a form of gas-mask fitted with oxygen cylinders. Two men, it is reported, died in trying to follow them.

Nothing could be seen of the Thetis this morn'

First To Safety— Back To Rescue

CAPTAIN F⸺ ⸺am, chief A⸺

⸺tandin⸺ ⸺ter when s⸺

SALV⸺E SHI⸺ TO ⸺Y TO ⸺ST NEW

---

was to warn off any ships that came too close to the area while the new submarine was being tested. The *Thetis* was due to make two test dives. The first would be a simple dive below the water level and straight back up again. The submarine would then make a second dive to about 60 feet.

Two other boats stood by just before it was time for the first test. They were waiting to take off most of the passengers from the submarine before the test started. There were 103 people on board the *Thetis*.

Lieutenant-Commander Bolus shouted across to the two boats to say that all the passengers had decided to stay on board for the test. The submarine and the tugboat had no radio contact, so the sailors on the tugboat had to watch the *Thetis* constantly to see what she was doing.

A signal came from the submarine that she was about to go down for her first test under the sea. It seemed to take some time for the submarine to go under. At last, she disappeared in a swirl of white foam.

The *Grebecock's* crew watched and waited. The submarine was supposed to return to the surface almost immediately, before doing the deeper test. The *Thetis* did not reappear. Without any radio contact, the *Grebecock* could only stand by and wait.

Eventually it became clear that something was wrong—the submarine should have surfaced hours before. The tugboat sent a signal about its worries to the navy base, many miles away.

By the time a number of ships had rushed to the scene and begun to search for the missing submarine, it was night. They had to wait until daybreak. It was not until about 7:30 A.M. the next day that a navy ship spotted the stern of the *Thetis* sticking out of the water.

To let people on the submarine know that help was coming, the boats on the surface made twelve small underwater explosions, At almost the same time, two exhausted men bobbed up in the water. They had swum up from the *Thetis*, taking the risk of getting out through the emergency hatch.

The soaking, tired men reported that everyone on board the submarine was alive but suffering badly from lack of air. Signals were sent from surrounding ships to the shore, to report that everyone on board was safe. More than 2,000 friends and relatives had been waiting for news. They were thrilled to hear that their loved ones were still alive.

There had been a flood in one of the torpedo tubes, sinking the bow and making the stern stick upwards. Two of the submarines six compartments were also flooded. The crew had fought to make the rest of the submarine watertight.

The two men who had escaped had been chosen as volunteers to take a message to the surface. They carried details of what had happened to the *Thetis* in a waterproof pouch, so that even if they died trying to get to the surface, the world would know what had happened.

On the surface, things were desperate. The rescuers knew that the people trapped inside the submarine would be running out of air. Signals were banged on the stern of the submarine to tell the people to get out by the escape hatch. This would not be easy.

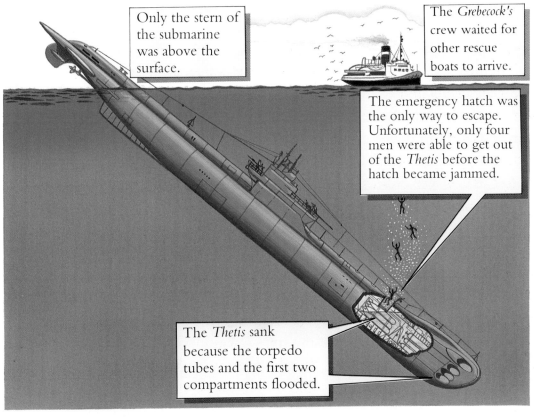

Only the stern of the submarine was above the surface.

The *Grebecock's* crew waited for other rescue boats to arrive.

LEFT This artist's impression of the Thetis *trapped underwater shows four men emerging from the escape hatch.*

The emergency hatch was the only way to escape. Unfortunately, only four men were able to get out of the *Thetis* before the hatch became jammed.

The *Thetis* sank because the torpedo tubes and the first two compartments flooded.

LEFT *During the long wait for news Mrs. Bolus, wife of the commanding officer of the* Thetis, *showed great courage trying to cheer up the other worried relatives waiting for news. Her husband died along with ninety-eight other men in the tragedy.*

WITNESS REPORT

THE AGONIZING WAIT

The situation was summed up by *The [London]Times* newspaper:

Up to a late hour last night it was still uncertain whether the officers and men on board the wrecked submarine Thetis *would enjoy a marvellous deliverance from deadly peril, or whether the Royal Navy would have to deplore one of the heaviest disasters it has ever suffered in a time of peace. No life was known to have been lost; but only four had actually been saved. A grim time limit overhung the rescue operations, and has now expired; for the air supply in the submarine was sufficient to last only until about 1:40 this morning.*

Source: *The [London] Times*, June 3, 1939.

They had to use special underwater breathing equipment. Four men tried to follow the first pair but one of them panicked when the hatch did not open and he pulled off the breathing equipment. All four men died. Two more men tried the escape and succeeded. They were very ill from lack of air but managed to tell the surface rescuers that more men would be trying to get out by the escape hatch.

However, it was too late. No more people managed to escape the stricken submarine. The air must have run out and the escape hatch had jammed after the last pair had escaped. Ninety-nine people died in the tragedy.

Today, such a terrible tragedy is unlikely to happen. Ways have been developed to attach air pipes to submarines, so that if people become trapped while under the surface they will not run out of air while waiting to be rescued. It is a great shame that such equipment was not available at the time of the *Thetis* tragedy.

THE SINKING OF THE *LUSITANIA*

On May 7, 1915, a German U-boat (a type of submarine) sank a huge passenger liner called the *Lusitania*. This event is thought by some to have changed history. A year before the sinking occurred, World War I (1914–18) had begun. Almost every European country was involved. Germany and Austria fought against Britain, France, and Russia.

The United States was not yet involved in the war. However, there were more than 200 Americans on board the *Lusitania* when she sank and many of them died. The American people were outraged by the attack.

This outrage later fueled the decision of the United States government to go to war against Germany and her allies in 1917, which changed the course of the war.

ABOVE The surprise attack from a German U-boat on the civilian passenger liner, Lusitania, *shocked the world.*

BELOW *A periscope was used to see above water level while the submarine remained below the surface.*
BELOW CENTER *The* Lusitania *was one of the fastest and most magnificent passenger liners of her day.*

NO WARNING GIVEN

At the time of the sinking of the *Lusitania*, neither side seemed to be winning the war in Europe. The Germans decided that to win the war they would have to keep important goods, such as food and the materials they needed to make weapons, from getting to Britain. These items were brought to Britain by sea, so the Germans started attacking British merchant ships.

Sailors on a merchant ship are not involved in warfare. For this reason international law says that an enemy must warn civilian and merchant ships before attacking, so the passengers and crew have time to leave the vessel in lifeboats.

This law was a problem for the Germans. British warships could travel faster than U-boats. So, if a U-boat warned a merchant ship that it was about to be attacked, a British warship could speed to the scene and destroy the U-boat. The German leaders told their U-boat captains that the international law was old-fashioned. They were not to issue warnings before they attacked any vessel.

THE UNBELIEVABLE THREAT

Some passengers who intended to sail on the *Lusitania* received telephone calls or telegrams warning them: "Have it on definite authority the *Lusitania* is to be torpedoed. You had better cancel passage immediately."

In American newspapers, an advertisement appeared from the German embassy warning that any British or British-allied ship might be destroyed.

Not one of the 218 American travelers canceled their passage because of the warnings, which were seen as bullying threats. Of the many who died in the disaster, 128 were Americans.

SURPRISE ATTACK

The *Lusitania* was a magnificent passenger liner and one of the fastest ships of her day. When she set sail on May 1, 1915 from New York, there were nearly 2,000 people on board. She made good progress across the Atlantic Ocean. One week later, sailing close to the coast of Ireland, the passengers looked forward to arriving in the English port of Liverpool in a few more hours. Little did they know, as they settled down to lunch, that a German U-boat was aiming to torpedo the *Lusitania*.

Only the periscope of the submarine showed above the water. It was impossible for the crew to see it.

Suddenly and without warning, two torpedoes were fired from the U-boat, ripping into the *Lusitania* and causing a huge explosion. A great pillar of water and

BELOW The Lusitania's *lookouts did not see the U-boat as it fired two torpedoes at the ship from only 650 feet away.*

First torpedo strike.

Third explosion occurred in the cargo hold.

Second torpedo strike.

shattered wood rose high into the sky. The ship's engines were damaged, which made it impossible to stop the ship. For what must have seemed an endless ten minutes the 31,000-ton steel liner rushed uncontrollably through the sea at more than 22 mph.

Most of the lifeboats could not be lowered because they had been smashed against the side of the ship as it raced out of control. Finally, the ship slowed down and the crew and passengers struggled to release some lifeboats and rafts. However, more than half of them could not be freed. There would not be enough room in the lifeboats for everybody on board.

Captain Turner remained on the bridge of the *Lusitania* to give orders for the safe evacuation of the passengers and crew. He stayed with his ship to the last. While those already in the lifeboats or in the water struggled to keep afloat, the *Lusitania* slid under the water—only 21 minutes after the torpedoes had struck. Many people were still on board.

Dozens of fishing boats and small craft rushed from the Irish coast to get to the scene of the disaster in answer to the *Lusitania*'s Mayday distress signal. Many people were saved, but 1,198 died in the disaster.

OPPOSITE *Newspaper reports of the sinking of the* Lusitania *shocked the public.*

WITNESS REPORT

A SURVIVOR'S STORY

Lady Mackworth, a survivor, was not able to get a place on a lifeboat and was still standing on the deck when the ship sank:

I suddenly felt the water all about me and was terrified lest I should be caught in something and held under. I went right under—a long way—and when I came to the surface I had swallowed a lot of water before I remembered to close my mouth tight. I was half unconscious, but I managed to seize a boat which I saw in front of me, and hang on to it. The water was crowded with wreckage…and people swimming…There were some boats not far away, and we all called to them, but the people in them could not hear us. I became unconscious, and the next thing I remember is lying on the deck of the Bluebell, *with a sailor bending over me saying, "You are better now."*

Source: *50 Great Disasters and Tragedies That Shocked the World—The Sinking of the* Lusitania by Christopher Swan (Published by Odhams Publishers).

ABOVE *Fishing boats, tugs, and every other available vessel rushed from the Irish coast to the scene of the disaster 30 miles from the shore.*

The Daily Mirror

CERTIFIED CIRCULATION LARGER THAN ANY OTHER PICTURE PAPER IN THE WORLD

No. 3,600. | Registered at the G.P.O. as a Newspaper. | SATURDAY, MAY 8, 1915 | 16 PAGES | One Halfpenny.

GIANT CUNARDER CROWDED WITH PASSENGERS CALLOUSLY SUNK WITHOUT WARNING OFF THE IRISH COAST.

COLLISION!

THE *TITANIC* DISASTER

Every year on April 14, a United States Coast Guard boat stops at a certain point in the icy Atlantic Ocean. So that the *Titanic* will never be forgotten, flowers are thrown into the sea. They mark the place where on a calm, clear night in April 1912, more than 1,500 lives were lost in one of the world's most dreadful sea disasters.

The *Titanic* was a fabulous, giant passenger liner ten decks high. The ship had luxurious furnishings. There was a huge ballroom as well as many fine dining rooms and lounges. The first-class cabins even had four-poster beds. A passenger could stroll around for over four miles exploring the wonders of this beautiful new ship.

ABOVE *Everyone thought the* Titanic *was unsinkable. It was a proud moment for the shipowners, the White Star Company, when she set sail on her maiden voyage.*

THE *TITANIC*

- 46,328 tons.
- 882 feet long.
- Three propellers.
- Top speed 29 mph.
- Engines capable of 46,000 horsepower.
- Space for 3,000 passengers.
- Twenty lifeboats with total space for 1,178 people.

OPPOSITE *In the darkness, the lookouts on the* Titanic *could not see the huge iceberg that lay directly in the ship's path.*

The *Titanic* was the pride of her owners, the White Star Company. She was called "the ship that could not sink." On her maiden voyage, the *Titanic* attracted many rich people who wanted to sail across the Atlantic Ocean from Britain to the United States on the safest, most superb ship of the time. Not all the passengers were rich, but even those traveling on the cheapest fare were well-fed and comfortable.

More than 2,200 travelers looked forward to the first ever voyage of the *Titanic* with great excitement. As the ship set sail on the afternoon of April 10, 1912, no one would have believed that only 711 of the passengers and crew would ever see land again.

BELOW The Titanic sailed from England, to France, then on to Ireland before making her ill-fated voyage across the North Atlantic Ocean.

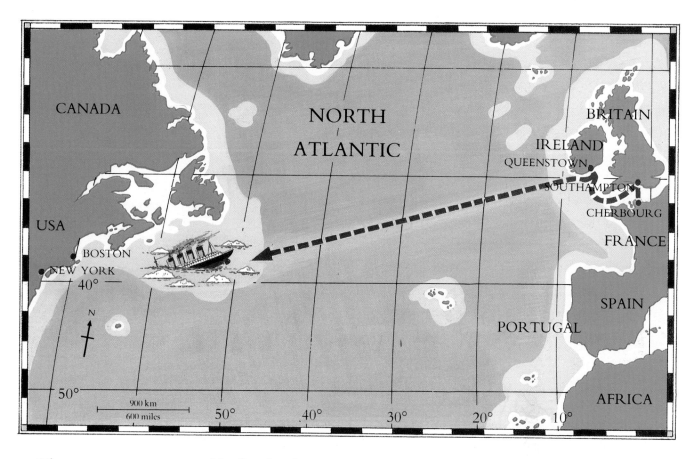

The voyage went smoothly for the first four days. On the night of Sunday, April 14, the *Titanic* slid easily through the calm seas of the North Atlantic Ocean. The lookouts up in the crow's nest watched the black sea and the clear sky. Close to midnight, a shocked lookout, Frederick Fleet, gave three sharp rings of the alarm bell to signal that an object was in the ship's path. "Iceberg right ahead!" he shouted, staring all the time at the massive, dark shape toward which they raced.

The warning came too late. The jagged iceberg ripped into the ship. It happened so quietly that Frederick Fleet thought it was just a scrape. "That was a narrow shave!" he cried with relief, as fragments of ice fell onto the deck. Down below, passenger Lawrence Beesley had just settled down to sleep. He noticed no more than a slight "dancing" movement from his bunk bed.

Unfortunately, Fleet was wrong. The collision was very serious. It was soon realized that the ship had been split open and was sinking. Captain Smith was called to the bridge as the true situation became clear. In less than two hours the *Titanic* would be completely underwater. When the captain called for the lifeboats to be lowered, a new horror unfolded. There was not going to be room in the lifeboats for everyone on board.

As the final lifeboats were lowered the stern lifted out of the water and the ship's lights, kept on by the brave efforts of the engineers, flashed and then went out forever. All the lifeboats were gone, but more than 1,500 people were still on board the sinking ship.

At 2 A.M. the ship swung around. Only the stern was visible, pointing straight up at the sky. She remained still for a moment, then slid to her final resting place on the seabed, more than two miles below the surface.

The *Titanic* had sunk by 2:10 A.M. Almost to the end, the brave wireless operators tapped out their signals for help to other boats, continuing long after Captain Smith had released them from their duties.

BELOW
An artist's impression of how the iceberg ripped a long gash into the Titanic *under the water level.*

Distress rockets were fired into the night sky.

The hull buckled from the impact of the collision.

TITANIC

The iceberg tore all the way through the double hull of the *Titanic*.

The underwater spur of the iceberg made a 300-foot gash below the water level.

ICEBERG

── WITNESS REPORT ──

WOMEN AND CHILDREN FIRST!

The wealthy American businessman Benjamin Guggenheim and his secretary Victor Giglio threw off their lifejackets and put on their finest evening clothes. Guggenheim explained:

We've dressed up in our best and are prepared to go down like gentlemen. Tell my wife, if it should happen that my secretary and I both go down, tell her I played the game out straight to the end. No woman shall be left aboard this ship because Ben Guggenheim is a coward.

Source: Titanic—*Triumph and Tragedy* by John P. Eaton and Charles A. Haas, (published by Patrick Stephens Ltd.).

RIGHT Women in a lifeboat prepare to be lowered into the icy sea to escape the doomed Titanic.

These tireless operators had managed to get a message through to the *Carpathia*, another passenger liner, 58 miles away across the hazardous waters:

Come at once. We have struck an iceberg. It's CQD, old man. Position 41° 46'N, 50° 14' W.

The *Carpathia* finally arrived at the *Titanic's* last position. There was nothing left where the grand ship had been. Slowly, in the dim light of dawn, the tragic events of the night became clear.

LEFT The exhausted wireless operator Jack Phillips continued to signal for help almost until the ship went down.

WITNESS REPORT

A SURVIVOR'S STORY

In the sea, a desperate struggle to survive now took place. Colonel Gracie of the United States army described the scene:

Dying men and women all around me were crying and moaning piteously. One of the Titanic's funnels separated and fell apart near me, scattering bodies in the water. I saw bodies everywhere, and all that came within reach I clung to.

He managed to struggle onto a raft: *Soon the raft became so full that it seemed as if she would sink if any more came on board her. The crew…therefore, had to refuse to permit any more to clamber on. This was the most pathetic and horrible sight of all. The piteous cries of those around us rose in my ears and I shall remember them until my dying day…Many of those whom we refused answered, as they went to their deaths, "Good luck! God bless you!"*

Source: *50 Great Disasters and Tragedies That Shocked The World—The Sinking of the* Titanic by Michael Geelan (published by Odhams Publishers).

ABOVE *This is a painting based on an eyewitness account of the* Titanic's *final moments.*

WITNESS REPORT

RACING TO THE RESCUE

The *Carpathia* rushed to get to the area. Captain Rostron described the journey:

More and more now we were keyed up. Icebergs loomed up and fell astern (behind); we never slackened, though sometimes we altered course suddenly to avoid them. It was an anxious time with the Titanic's fateful experience very close in our minds. There were 700 souls on Carpathia; these lives, as well as all the survivors of Titanic herself, depended on a sudden turn of the wheel.

Source: *50 Great Disasters and Tragedies That Shocked The World—The Sinking of the* Titanic by Michael Geelan (published by Odhams Publishers).

Shivering survivors were plucked from the crowded lifeboats. A total of 711 had lived to be rescued by the *Carpathia*. More than double that number had died in the freezing sea.

After the disaster, an investigation was held to find out why the tragedy had occurred. This led to improvements in laws about safety at sea. From then on, ships had to carry enough lifeboats for all their passengers and have radio systems. The coast guards set up regular ice patrols, using boats and aircraft to warn ships of danger and to prevent such a terrible disaster from ever happening again.

BELOW Sketches of the Titanic's final hours based on eyewitness accounts an artist heard aboard the Carpathia.

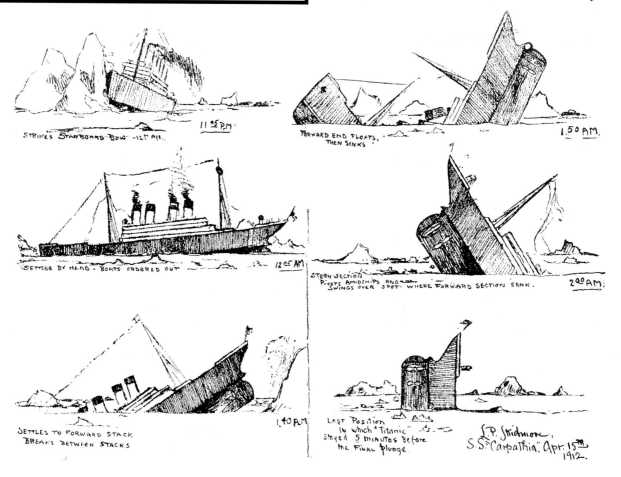

STRIKES STARBOARD BOW -11.45 PM. 11.45 PM.

FORWARD END FLOATS, THEN SINKS. 1.50 AM.

SETTLES BY HEAD - BOATS ORDERED OUT 12.05 AM.

STERN SECTION PIVOTS AMIDSHIPS AND SWINGS OVER SPOT WHERE FORWARD SECTION SANK. 2.00 AM.

SETTLES TO FORWARD STACK BREAKS BETWEEN STACKS 1.40 AM.

LAST POSITION IN WHICH "TITANIC" STAYED 5 MINUTES BEFORE THE FINAL PLUNGE.

S.P. Stridmore, S.S. "Carpathia" Apr. 15th 1912.

FIRE ON BOARD!

Fire is a terrible threat to a ship. It may seem strange that a vessel surrounded by water would catch fire, but there are many reasons why this can happen.

A MYSTERIOUS BLAZE

The *Morro Castle* was a passenger ship on the last leg of its journey from Havana, Cuba, to New York. On the evening of September 7, 1934, Captain Robert Wilmott died suddenly under mysterious circumstances. Then another strange event occurred—a fire broke out on board the ship early the next morning. The cause of the fire has never been found, but it may have been started on purpose.

ABOVE The haunting sight of the stricken passenger ship, the Morro Castle—*still ablaze and with smoke billowing from her decks—while beached off the shore of New Jersey.*

It was 2:30 A.M. on September 8 and the ship was only eight miles from the shore when someone noticed the fire.

Many passengers were asleep in their cabins when flames started to race through the wood-paneled ship. Proper fire-fighting equipment was not at hand and the fire took hold quickly. Even though the ship was so close to shore, more than 134 people died in the blaze.

WITNESS REPORT

A SURVIVOR'S STORY

A survivor, Dr. Charles S. Cochrane, described the scene in the *New York Times:*

I was awakened from a sound sleep, at just what time I don't know, by clouds of suffocating smoke filling my cabin…At almost the same time someone banged and hammered at my cabin door and shouted something unintelligible.

Confused by my sudden awakening, and choking and unable to see because of the dense smoke in the cabin, I tried vainly to find the door. Just in time my groping hands came in contact with a porthole. I crawled through it and dropped to the deck outside.

ABOVE *News reporters and film crews watch as police officers carry victims and survivors from the* Morro Castle *off one of the rescue ships at New York's docks.*

There was no apparent panic. The crew was making frantic efforts to launch the boats. All the time the flames were creeping nearer.

Suddenly someone gave me a violent push and I half fell and half staggered into the lifeboat. There was trouble in launching it, and it seemed almost a half-hour before we were in the water and pulling away from the Morro Castle. *The front of the ship was a pillar of flame by this time.*

Source: *New York Times,* September 9, 1934.

FERRY ON FIRE – THE *DOÑA PAZ*

Oil is a fuel that can cause terrible fires. On December 21, 1987 the dangerously overcrowded *Doña Paz* ferry collided with an oil tanker carrying 8,800 barrels of oil near the Philippine Islands in Southeast Asia. As the two vessels collided, the oil caught fire and spread over both ships. The people trapped on board could only escape by jumping into the sea—which was covered in burning oil and full of sharks. The death toll is believed to be over 1,530—even more than were lost on the *Titanic* in 1912.

BELOW RIGHT People gather at a dock in the Philippines to hear news of friends and relatives who were on the Doña Paz ferry at the time of the accident.

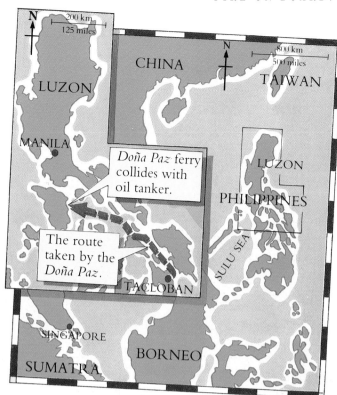

Doña Paz ferry collides with oil tanker.

The route taken by the *Doña Paz*.

ABOVE This map shows the position where the Doña Paz ferry disaster happened.

WITNESS REPORT

A SURVIVOR'S STORY

Mr. Paquito Osabel described in *The [London] Times* how he escaped:

I was sleeping when I heard an explosion. I looked out and saw another ship was on fire. In just two seconds there was a big fire on our ship and I heard everybody screaming and wailing.

The fire spread rapidly and engulfed our ship. There were flames everywhere. People were screaming and jumping. The smoke was terrible. We couldn't see each other and it was dark.

I could see flames in the water below, but I jumped anyway.'

Mr. Osabel said he clung to a plank and swam for more than an hour before being picked up by another ship.

Source: *The [London] Times*, December 22, 1987.

THE *PIPER ALPHA* DISASTER

Fire at sea does not only affect sailing vessels. To get oil from rocks beneath the seabed, an oil rig has to be built on top of the oil well. There are three types of oil rigs used at sea. Fixed and movable rigs go down to the seabed. A floating oil rig does not go down to the bottom of the sea.

In 1988, there was a disastrous fire on the *Piper Alpha* oil rig. It was an American-owned fixed oil rig, sited 120 miles off the coast of Scotland in the North Sea. As well as pumping out more than 150,000 barrels of oil a day, the rig also provided a huge source of natural gas. The platform on the oil rig acted as a huge factory, separating oil and gas that was piped up from the seabed.

Suddenly, on the night of July 6, 1988, the two fuels exploded together, causing a huge ball of fire on the platform. The flames leaped 400 feet into the air. The heat was so intense that the massive metal girders and the

MAIN PICTURE A support platform fights the flames on the Piper Alpha *oil rig.*

RIGHT The Piper Alpha *oil rig was still burning two days after the explosion. The massive metal structure was buckled and twisted by the incredible heat from the fire.*

framework of the oil rig began to buckle and topple into the sea. The oil workers on the rig were trapped in a horrifying situation. The only chance of survival was to jump over into the icy-cold sea. Of the 166 oil workers on board *Piper Alpha* only 65 survived.

Safety rules on oil rigs are being improved constantly. Better still, ways are being found to use robots to do as many jobs as possible on the oil rigs, so that there will be fewer people actually working on the platforms. However, drilling for oil will always be an extremely dangerous job.

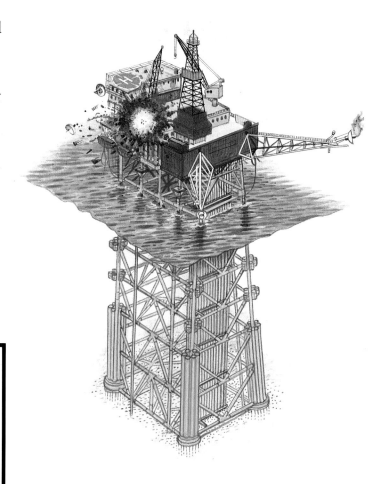

WITNESS REPORT

FACE FLAMES OR LEAP INTO THE SEA

Roy Carey was working on the platform when the first explosion occurred:

There was just a mass of smoke. There was no time to ask. It was over the side or nothing. I just dived in. It may have been 18 meters [60 feet]. I was totally enveloped. It was a case of fry and die, or jump and try.

Roy jumped without thinking. This is how he described the scene in the water:

The flames were billowing above us. I found my head was being cooked and I had to keep ducking down to get it cool.

He and three others clung to the wreck of a lifeboat until they were rescued.

Source: *The Daily Telegraph*, July 8, 1988.

RIGHT The Piper Alpha *oil rig was destroyed by the fire that followed a massive explosion.*

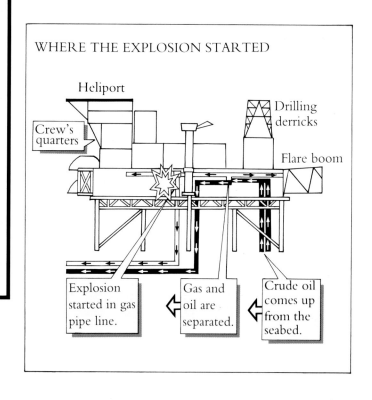

WHERE THE EXPLOSION STARTED

Heliport

Crew's quarters

Drilling derricks

Flare boom

Explosion started in gas pipe line.

Gas and oil are separated.

Crude oil comes up from the seabed.

OIL SPILL DISASTERS

Sea disasters do not create only human tragedies. They can be disastrous for all kinds of marine wildlife as well.

Huge amounts of oil are shipped around the world every day. The cheapest way to ship oil across the oceans is to use massive oil tankers. These "supertankers" are often so big that crews use bicycles to get from one end to the other. A supertanker can hold more than 250,000 tons of oil, so a single oil spill can be a major disaster.

One type of sea accident that has been the cause of several of the world's worst oil tanker disasters is called "stranding." This is when a ship ends up with its bottom caught on rocks or a sandbank. It usually happens because of human error by the captain or the navigator.

STRANDED

In 1967, a stranding took place that was to warn the world about the dangers of all oil-carrying tankers. At that time, the *Torrey Canyon* was the world's thirteenth largest sea vessel. Today she would only be considered a medium-sized tanker, because bigger vessels are built all the time.

The *Torrey Canyon* was near the end of her journey bringing oil from Kuwait, in the Middle East, to an oil refinery in Wales. The tanker was trying to pass the western tip of Cornwall in England. To save time, she took a short cut around an area of rocks called the Seven Stones.

ABOVE *After being stranded for days the huge oil tanker,* Torrey Canyon, *broke in two—releasing even more oil into the sea.*

The ship was being steered by the automatic pilot. She was getting close to hazardous rocks but the crew was too late in taking over the steering to miss them. The *Torrey Canyon* scraped over a rock at Seven Stones, ripping a 650-foot tear in her side. The ship was firmly stuck on top of the rock. Immediately, her cargo of oil started to seep into the sea.

No one was quite sure how to deal with the damaged ship. For ten days the tanker was battered by the sea; it eventually broke in two. As everyone argued about what to do, the damage got worse. The oil slick spread over 700 square miles of the sea, threatening the shores of Britain and France with a dark, sticky slime.

The British government started an expensive operation to try to break up the oil by mixing it up with millions of gallons of detergent. More than 4,000 people were involved in trying to contain the oil slick at sea and 2,000 more fought it from the land.

Eventually, the *Torrey Canyon* broke up completely and all of her 131,500-ton cargo of oil drifted into the sea. The crew was removed and the Royal Air Force bombed the ship 40 times, trying to set fire to the oil. It was thought that if the oil was burned on the sea, it would cause less damage to the environment. The sea water kept putting out the flames so this did not work. While this was happening, the oil spill spread farther.

WITNESS REPORT

THE BLACKENED SEA

In *The [London]Times* newspaper, journalist Julian Mounter described the scene just after it had happened:

For a few miles southwest of Land's End [Cornwall] the seascape was filthy with oil; it varies in color from a dark streaky blue to a thick and pale brown.

Everywhere is the sickening smell. After a while, one can taste oil. Spotted around are the dead birds; only a few but they are the first of possibly hundreds.

Source: *The [London] Times*, March 18, 1967.

RIGHT Many people helped with the cleanup operation after the Torrey Canyon *spill near Cornwall in 1967. These boys rescued birds whose feathers were covered in oil.*

HOW OIL HARMS MARINE WILDLIFE

Oil spills harm animals living in or near the sea. If a bird's feathers become covered in oil, it cannot fly or keep warm. When animals such as seals have their fur covered in oil, they lose warmth from their coats. As animals try to clean the oil off their bodies, they swallow it and damage their stomachs. After they breathe in the poisonous fumes from the oil, they cannot breathe normally. The affected animals almost always die a slow and painful death.

In the sea itself, fish and their food are poisoned and a layer of thick tar forms on the seabed, which kills all the creatures and plants it covers.

BELOW A bird covered in oil cannot fly or keep warm. Millions of birds have died as the result of oil spills from supertankers.

BELOW The area affected by the Exxon Valdez *oil spill.*

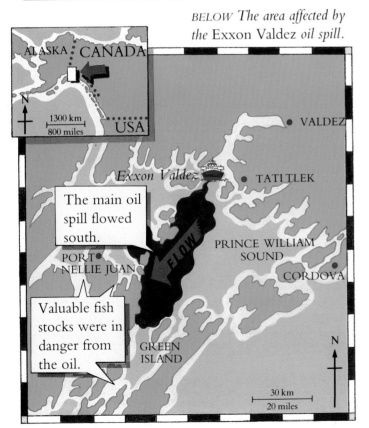

The main oil spill flowed south.

Valuable fish stocks were in danger from the oil.

The cleanup operation along the south coast of England and some parts of the northern French coast took months and cost a huge sum of money.

One man lost his life during an attempt to salvage the *Torrey Canyon,* but this was not the only loss. Around 100,000 seabirds were affected by the oil, many of which died. The loss of so much marine wildlife and the cost of the operation showed what was in store for the future, as oil tankers continued to get bigger and bigger.

THE *EXXON VALDEZ* DISASTER

There have been several disastrous oil tanker strandings since the *Torrey Canyon.* In 1978, the *Amoco Cadiz* tanker crashed onto rocks near the French shore. This spill was around

1.3 million barrels of oil—nearly twice the amount carried by the *Torrey Canyon*. During the 1970s and 1980s there were also serious spills off the coast of California and in the Gulf of Mexico.

On March 24, 1989, another oil disaster shocked the world. The *Exxon Valdez*, a 987-foot tanker, hit a rock in the crystal clear waters of Prince William Sound, Alaska. Two-hundred-forty-thousand barrels of oil blackened the bay, making it the largest spill in United States waters.

CLEANING UP OIL SPILLS

There are a number of ways to deal with oil spills in the sea. Each, though, has its drawbacks.

If an oil spill is left alone, eventually the sea will break it up. However, by then it will have caused a great deal of harm to wildlife, and even years later sticky balls of tar will show up on beaches.

Detergents can break up the oil, but they also pollute the sea and coast with poisons that can kill sea life.

At first, the oil lies on the surface of the sea, so floating barriers can be put in the water to keep it from spreading. If the sea is calm, sometimes the oil can be sucked into another tanker using pumps and suction hoses. Another calm-weather cure is to try to soak up the oil in materials such as straw or peat and then remove the oily material.

Oil can be made to sink by covering it with powdered chalk, but then the oil will end up damaging the seabed.

All these cleanup operations cost a lot of money and sometimes do not even work.

LEFT *Another ship is brought alongside the* Exxon Valdez *to try to transfer some of the stricken ship's remaining oil.*

BELOW *Floating barriers are put in the sea in an attempt to keep oil spills from spreading any farther.*

Because oil spills ruin the marine environment, much effort is going into preventing these disasters by designing safer tankers.

Oil companies are beginning to build tankers with double hulls. These ships have two outer layers and two bottoms. If the outer hull is damaged by collision or grounding, then the inner hull prevents the oil from being spilled. After the *Exxon*

Valdez disaster, the United States government has said that it will at some time in the future require all oil tankers to have double hulls. The process of changing to new, safer ships is both slow and costly. But whatever safety measures are adopted, shipping oil will always be risky.

OPPOSITE The half-sunken Amoco Cadiz *tanker, which crashed on to rocks off the French coast, causing a huge oil spill in 1978.*

WITNESS REPORT

THE BLACK WAVE

Here is how journalist George Gordon described the *Exxon Valdez* spill in the *Daily Mail*:

A black wave of death swept along the Alaskan coastline last night. It wiped out fish, birds, and the feeding grounds of tens of millions of salmon. "I think it's quite clear now," said Richard Devens, mayor of the town of Valdez, "our area is faced with the destruction of our entire way of life."

Source: *Daily Mail*, March 25, 1989.

BELOW The Exxon Valdez *disaster had one of the most expensive and longest cleanup operations to date.*

DEATH BY DESIGN?

During World War II (1939–45) a new craft, called the "landing ship," was designed so that tanks and trucks could be driven straight onto land from the ship. The craft had loading doors in the bow that opened out so that a ramp could be laid down on the land. This speeded up loading and unloading in dangerous waters.

This design made the landing ship very unsafe because it meant that one of the decks of the ship did not have a separate watertight area. This meant that if one of the loading doors burst open during a journey, water could rush in and flood the whole deck area. Once water is allowed to move freely across a large area of a ship, it can make the ship roll from side to side and possibly capsize.

A ship can capsize within minutes. This means that if an accident happens there may

OPPOSITE
The Herald of Free Enterprise *lying helpless in the water.*

RIGHT The ferry's open loading doors can be seen clearly in this photograph.

be no time to lower lifeboats or put on lifejackets.

After the war, some of these landing ships started to be used as an easy way to transport vehicles and passengers between islands on short trips. By the 1960s, the design for these landing ships was used for big car and passenger ferries all over the world. They were called "ro-ros," which stood for "roll-on, roll-off."

THE *HERALD OF FREE ENTERPRISE* TRAGEDY

On March 7, 1987, the *Herald of Free Enterprise* car and passenger ferry set sail from Zeebrugge harbor in Belgium, heading for Dover, England. As the ferry pulled out to the mouth of the harbor everything seemed to be normal.

The sea was calm, the wind was light, and the evening clear. There should have been no problem with the crossing, but, only eight minutes after Captain Lewry launched the ferry, it suddenly lurched sideways. The giant steel loading doors had not been shut properly. The sea began to pour into a car deck that was the size of a football field. The *Herald of Free Enterprise* had no chance of remaining afloat once that open area began to flood. The captain only had time to send a Mayday signal.

The passengers had no warning of the nightmare ahead of them. Once the ferry had capsized many of the passenger decks began to flood. People were thrown into a panic, scrambling around in the dark—desperate to hold on to their loved ones and to get out.

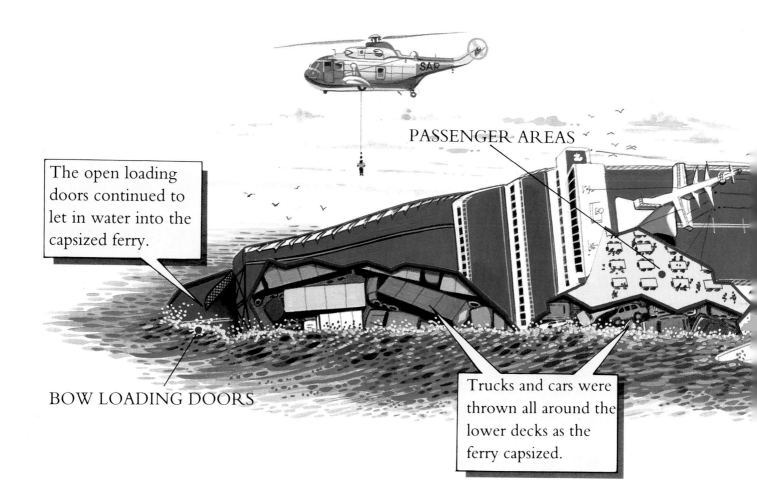

The open loading doors continued to let in water into the capsized ferry.

PASSENGER AREAS

BOW LOADING DOORS

Trucks and cars were thrown all around the lower decks as the ferry capsized.

ABOVE The grim rescue operation taking place on the Herald of Free Enterprise.

As soon as the accident happened an international rescue operation began. Rescue boats were at the scene in minutes. Various fishing boats and navy ships in the area rushed to Zeebrugge harbor. The rescuers worked for hours taking survivors off the ferry and to the safety of the shore. At the end of the operation, 409 people had been rescued, but tragically 136 people had died in the terrible disaster.

The International Maritime Organization has been trying to make car and passenger ferries safer. New ships must be built with more watertight sections. If a ferry starts to flood, these sections will keep it upright long enough for passengers and crew to make an

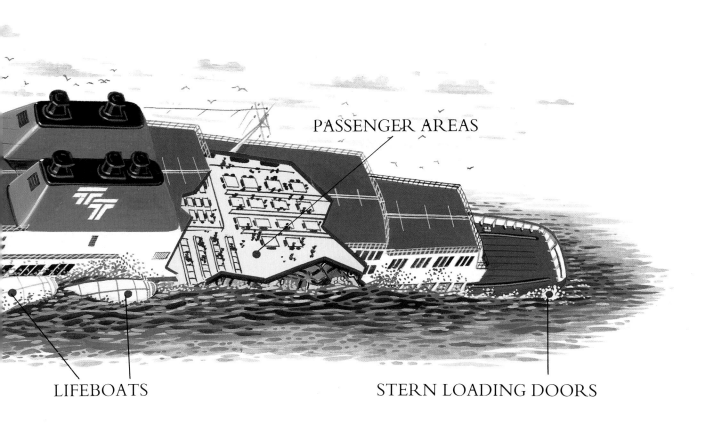

PASSENGER AREAS

LIFEBOATS

STERN LOADING DOORS

emergency exit. Older ships will eventually have to be changed to make them more watertight.

There are many people who have survived sea disasters. There are also many who have lost friends or relatives in such tragedies. It can be very hard for people to recover and get back to ordinary life after experiencing the horror of a major disaster.

However, it should also be remembered that the chances of becoming involved in a disaster are still very, very small. It can only be hoped that with every mistake that has cost human life, a lesson has been learned that will prevent other disasters.

ABOVE A survivor of the Herald of Free Enterprise *throwing flowers into the sea near the wreck.*

45

GLOSSARY

Automatic pilot   A special computer on a ship that will steer the ship on a preplanned route.

Bow   The front part of a ship or submarine.

Bridge   The control area of a ship that holds the steering equipment.

Capsize   Turn over in the water.

Cargo   The goods that an airplane, ship, or truck carries.

Civilizations   Large groups of people who live in societies that have certain rules and customs.

CQD   A radio distress signal that stood for CQ (all stations) D (danger). This signal was replaced by the SOS signal that is known all over the world.

Crow's nest   The highest part of a ship where lookouts can watch for any danger.

Decks   Different floors on a ship, such as the upper deck or lower deck.

Diesel engine   A type of engine that works using diesel oil (a kind of refined gasoline).

Embassy   A headquarters for the representatives of one country who live in another country. These representatives look after the interests of their country of origin.

Funnels   The tall towers on a ship that let out hot air, smoke, and steam.

Hull   The main framework of a boat.

Maiden voyage   A ship's first trip.

Mayday   A distress call that is made over a radio and is known all over the world.

Merchant ships   Vessels that carry goods, such as food and machinery, around the world. The crews are called merchant sailors.

Ocean liner   A large passenger ship.

Oil rig   A construction used for drilling for oil, gas, and other materials found below the ground or seabed.

Periscope   A tube with mirrors placed inside it used for seeing things around corners. Submarine periscopes are very powerful and are built into the main turret of the vessel.

Porthole   A watertight window in the side of a vessel.

Salvaged   When items have been found and brought to a safe place.

Stern   The back part of a ship or submarine.

Torpedo   A missile (bomb) that is fired by a submarine through special tubes.

Underwater robot   A special machine that can go down to great depths in the sea to help with research or to find wreckage.

Vessel   Any kind of ship.

FURTHER READING

Ardley, Neil. *Oil Rigs*. Ada Ok.: Garrett, 1990.

Ballard, Robert D. *Exploring the Titanic*. New York: Scholastic, 1991.

Carr, Terry. *Spill! The Story of the* Exxon Valdez. New York: Franklin Watts, 1991.

Carter, Katherine. *Ships and Seaports*. Chicago: Childrens Press, 1982.

Humble, Richard. *U-Boat*. New York: Franklin Watts, 1990.

Thomas, David A. *How Ships Are Made*. New York: Facts on File, 1989.

Tunis, Edwin. *Oars, Sails and Steam: A Picture Book of Ships*. New York: HarperCollins, 1977.

ACKNOWLEDGMENTS
Quote appearing on page 30: copyright © 1934 by the New York Times Company. Reprinted by permission.
Quote appearing on page 40: copyright © the Source/Solo.

PICTURE ACKNOWLEDGMENTS
Mary Evans Picture Library 5, 7, 17, 18 (top), 20, 22, 26 (top); John Frost Historical Newspaper Service 14, 16; Photri 18-19; Popperfoto 29, 35; Rex Features Ltd 13, 23 (Sachs), 31 (Aral), 32-33, 39 (M. Ginies), 40 (Schultz/Orth), 41, 43 (Fraser/Lafaille), 44 (Delahaye/Ouaki); Syndication International Ltd 8-9, 11; Topham *cover* (inset), 8 (bottom), 10, 12, 28, 30, 32, 36, 37, 38-39, 42, 45; Tony Stone Worldwide *cover* (background) (A. Husmo), 4-5 (H. Johnston); WPL 21, 25, 26 (bottom), 27 (ILN); ZEFA 6.
All illustrations are by Tony Jackson.

INDEX